A Pause in the Symphony

In the grand play of life, we pause,
A rubber chicken's final applause.
The conductor's lost, can't find his place,
So we dance in circles, a goofy embrace.

With violins playing an off-key tune,
The tuba's grumbling, 'give me a spoon.'
We twirl like the leaves in a whimsical spree,
As laughter and chaos collide with glee.

Original title:
Stems of Stillness

Copyright © 2025 Creative Arts Management OÜ
All rights reserved.

Author: Alexander Thornton
ISBN HARDBACK: 978-1-80567-031-5
ISBN PAPERBACK: 978-1-80567-111-4

Threads of Stillness

Threading through moments, quite absurd,
A cat wearing socks, such a sight deferred.
It lounges in comfort, claims every chair,
While we trip on the yarn, unaware of despair.

The clock ticks slowly, it's tickled by time,
A snail contemplates if it's worth the climb.
Each pause is a giggle, a chance to unwind,
As silliness lingers, a pattern unkind.

The Beauty of the Unhurried

Oh, the art of being splendidly late,
Like a tortoise wearing a fancy neck gait.
With ice cream that melts before it's a treat,
We savor the moments, far more than the heat.

A squirrel in a dapper little bow tie,
Chasing its tail with a fervent sigh.
For why rush the fun, when joy can expand,
With pancakes that flip from the cozy hand.

A Quiet Awakening

As morning creeps in with a sleepy face,
The puppy's deep yawn gives the day a grace.
With cereal floating like boats on a sea,
We giggle at life's little absurdity.

The sun peeks through cracks in the curtain's weave,
A sock on the ceiling makes us believe.
In the calm of the chaos, we find our delight,
A quiet awakening, a funny goodnight.

Hushed Harmonies

In a garden where whispers play,
The daisies wear hats on a sunny day.
Bumblebees perform their soft ballet,
While the squirrels scheme to steal the hay.

Leaves confide in murmurs low,
As daisies gossip in a row.
Pigeons tweet jokes, quite the show,
And all around, the breezes blow.

Shadows of Serenity

Under the moon, where shadows prance,
The crickets hold a midnight dance.
Frogs croak tunes, as if by chance,
And fireflies twirl in a twinkly trance.

Cats sit proudly, their tails held high,
Winking at stars like they own the sky.
A hedgehog grins, "Oh me, oh my!"
As night unfolds its soft lullaby.

Ripples of Quiet Reflection

The pond reflects a clownish frog,
Who leaps in style, like a dog on a log.
Turtles chuckle, quite a dialogue,
As dragonflies spin in a sunny smog.

A silver fish jumps with a splashy wit,
And laughs at her friend who's quite a bit split.
"Is that a joke, or just a skit?"
As nature boasts of its quirky grit.

The Weight of Breath

In the stillness, whispers take flight,
A sleepy badger mumbles at night.
While leaves discuss who's dizzy with fright,
Slow snails carry their homes, what a sight!

Breezes laugh, tickling aged trees,
Mice offer acorns to buzzing bees.
In this world, where laughter agrees,
The quiet hums, like a gentle tease.

Echoes of a Whispered Dream

In the quiet of the night, cats dance with glee,
Tales of mice and moonbeams, a shadowy spree.
A dreamer snores loudly, a symphony proclaims,
While the bedbugs are tap dancing, playing silly games.

A rubber chicken quacks, in a hall of sleepy heads,
Snoozing folks and wild dreams, tangled up in beds.
The pillows engage in debates, who's fluffier than whom,

As laughter drifts softly in the warm little room.

Traces of Time's Embrace

Tick-tock with a twist, clocks wearing bright hats,
A snail writes a novel, as slow as the brats.
Tea kettles scream loudly, 'You're wasting my steam!'
While socks in the dryer conspire to scheme.

Time waltzes in slippers, making quite the fuss,
As coffee spills secrets in a very loud husk.
The calendar giggles, on the wall it does dwell,
Counting each day like it's a merry little spell.

Beneath the Surface

Underwater turtles, hold a grand parade,
While fish wear top hats, and dancers charade.
Crabs hold a contest for the fanciest pin,
As the seaweed grows jealous, wishing to win.

A bubble took flight, like a balloon on a spree,
It whispered sweet nothings to a clam by the sea.
Octopus chefs stir up a tempestuous brew,
While plankton are giggling at the jokes they knew.

Reflections of the Heart

Mirrors chuckle quietly, as faces come and go,
They hold secrets of laughter, and a hint of woe.
A heart sits on a sofa, knitting dreams with flair,
While socks, mismatched and eager, dance anywhere.

A wink from the moon, as shadows jump and play,
Reflections of beat hearts, in a silly ballet.
The whispers of sweet yearning find comfort in the air,
As giggles echo softly, love's tender snare.

Silence Speaks

In the garden where whispers grow,
The rabbits gossip, taking it slow.
A snail holds court, its shell a throne,
While daisies nod in secrets unknown.

Chirping crickets start a jazz band,
Wags the dog, on his paws he stands.
The breeze tells tales of a wandering cat,
While frogs croak humor, like they're all that.

The clouds above giggle, drifting wide,
As butterflies dance, no place to hide.
Leaves share a chuckle, with roots intertwined,
Nature's own laughter, endlessly designed.

When silence strikes, it's a punchline bold,
As the sun sets, in hues of gold.
Life's quiet moments, a comedic peak,
In giggles and grins, the stillness speaks.

Whispered Secrets of the Night

The moon tripped over a cloud's sheer lace,
It laughed at owls with a jolly face.
Stars played tag in the velvety skies,
While crickets rehearsed for their nighttime cries.

A breeze swept by, looking quite aloof,
Tickled the trees, causing quite the goof.
Frogs wore bowties in the marshy dew,
They croaked their jokes, 'Why not join the queue?'

The Palette of Silence

In the quiet, colors danced out of sync,
Green giggled loud while blue winks and thinks.
Yellow spilled sunshine on sleepy old walls,
Red played hide and seek, bouncing off stalls.

Brushes dipped in whispers, so bold and bright,
Painted the world's secrets by soft candlelight.
Each stroke a secret, each color a laugh,
Even the shadows wished to join in the craft.

Unseen Crossroads

Two paths once met in a tangle of weeds,
Both wearing hats and disguising their needs.
One said, 'This way leads to the culinary feast!'
The other blinked back, 'But I'll have the least!'

Squirrels debated on nutty affairs,
While the grass whispered gossip about fuzzy bears.
A traffic jam of butterflies blocked the sun,
And giggles erupted as they all tried to run.

Breaths of Time

A tick-tock laughed from a clock on the wall,
Each second a scoop at the funfair's call.
Time tried to roller skate, legs all askew,
It tripped on a tick and fell right on cue!

Calendar days played hopscotch in glee,
Shuffling through pages with timeless esprit.
They tossed confetti, each month a new rhyme,
Sipping on giggles, they brewed up good time!

The Language of Unwatched Hours

In the clutches of a clock,
Time tiptoes like a sock.
Tick-tock giggles in the air,
Whispers secrets without a care.

Coffee brews a silent song,
Mugs dance, they can't be wrong.
Sugar cubes take to the sky,
Laughter echoes, oh my, oh my!

Lost socks have a party vibe,
Chasing shadows, they'd inscribe.
Meanwhile, the cat stops to ponder,
Life's a joke, who needs to wander?

Mismatched forks join in delight,
As pancakes flip in sheer delight.
Hours unwind like silly string,
Unwatched hours do their thing!

Garden of Forgotten Echoes

In a patch where giggles grow,
Whispers hang like misty glow.
Flowers wave with cheeky flair,
Sunshine tickles, unaware.

A snail dreams of speedy feats,
Orchestras play with fuzzy beats.
Laughter blooms in every nook,
Even the mud has stories, look!

Garden gnomes perform ballet,
Under moonlight, they sway and play.
Bugs wear hats, they take the limelight,
In this space, all's not quite right.

Each rock holds a memory dear,
Old shoes chant their tales, oh dear!
Quiet giggles in the breeze,
Ticklish whispers among the trees.

The Weight of Quietude

In a room where silence snores,
Lazily opening hidden doors.
Cushions giggle while they sit,
Moderate chaos, just a bit.

Socks argue about the heat,
While chairs form a secret fleet.
Whispers float like lazy cats,
Each corner holds a thousand chats.

Dust bunnies plot a revolution,
They demand snacks and a solution.
Tickles from the air arise,
Even silence sometimes lies.

A book winks, it's in on the joke,
In stillness, it softly spoke.
Capturing joys we try to hide,
In the hush, all fun resides.

Embracing the Invisible Flow

Time's a river made of fudge,
Swimming in warmth, we never budge.
Drifting lazily like a wink,
Here, we pause and start to think.

Leaves dance like confetti petals,
Each twist whispers funny metals.
Clouds share stories, giggle loud,
In the hush, we are the crowd.

Waves of laughter gently poke,
Invisible socks start to croak.
Footsteps echo, soft and merry,
In this flow, we take a cherry.

Time's a friend that skips and spins,
In laughter, we all dive in.
Embraced by joy's playful scheme,
Dancing along in a silly dream.

Serenade of the Solitude

In the quiet, a snail races,
Mollusk with dreams in slow traces.
A turtle as coach shakes its head,
"Speed up, buddy! Or you'll just be dead!"

The cushions are plotting a coup,
They're tired of folks plopping anew.
A lone sock hops, seeking its mate,
While a goldfish is contemplating fate.

A cactus sings songs of the night,
With prickles that twinkle in light.
It sways without rhythm or beat,
Craving some sunlight, but life tastes sweet.

The cat naps with profound grace,
While the dust bunnies dance in their place.
"Is there food?" says the lazy old chair,
"I'm just here for the comfort, I swear!"

Still Lifes of Thought

The teapot dreams of spouts and steeps,
While the fridge hums, secrets it keeps.
A banana in pajamas, quite bold,
Sings of the warmth from the sun, oh so gold.

Face down, the book had a fight,
With coffee stains blotting its insight.
"Oh, help!" cried the pencil, quite mad,
"It's hard to write when I'm feeling so bad!"

Dust motes dance in the sunlight's grip,
Each one a star on a mini road trip.
A sock puppet whispers in dread,
"Did you hear what the blanket just said?"

The clock ticks on, ignoring the chase,
While time plays hide-and-seek in its space.
The paperclip dreams of grand things,
But finds only daily tasks that it brings.

Murmurs of the Mind

Inside the brain, a party can rise,
With neurons dancing, oh what a surprise!
A thought bubble bursts with a pop,
Sending ideas flying, then they drop.

A daydream wants to take a trip,
But the alarm clock gives it a slip.
"Just five more minutes, please!" it pleads,
"To plant my thoughts like garden seeds!"

The fridge debated a midnight snack,
While socks played tag, both white and black.
A mind map spins in delightful loops,
As the coffee pot brews a dream of groups.

Scribbles turn into a concert hall,
Each doodle a singer, standing tall.
The eraser blushes, busting with pride,
While paper hoards secrets it cannot hide.

Threads of Peace

In the quiet of the evening light,
A spider spins without a fright.
It crafts a web, a glittering dance,
As the world below misses its chance.

The blanket's warmth, a gentle tease,
Offers comfort and a soft breeze.
While the lamp shades whisper to the floor,
"Shall we host a shadowy encore?"

A pizza slice dreams of toppings galore,
While plates argue who was used before.
The napkin flies, preparing a toast,
To the coasters who guard drinks coast to coast.

All is calm on this cozy stage,
As the cat reads a book, turns the page.
Tickling laughter floats in the air,
While the clock gives a knowing glare.

Solitary Melodies

In the corner sits a shoe,
It grumbles soft, 'Where's my crew?'
With dust bunnies as its friends,
They start a jam that never ends.

A snail just slid across the floor,
With a trumpet made of candy core.
The echo laughs, it's all a game,
Yet here we are, still feeling fame.

Harmonics of the Unhurried

A turtle strums a lazy tune,
Ignoring all, beneath the moon.
A feathered choir sings along,
The rhythm's slow but never wrong.

A cat conducts with floppy ears,
Each purr releases hidden cheers.
The sun, it yawns, the sky turns pink,
And all the stars just stop to think.

Tides of Interior Calm

A goldfish dreams of ocean waves,
Bobbling thoughts in glassy caves.
Its wish to swim off in a spree,
Yet floats instead in peaceful glee.

A couch potato in a chair,
Strategizes, "I'll get up… where?"
But snacks are close; it can't resist,
And so it lounges in blissful mist.

The Space Between Words

A penguin pondering on the ice,
Thinks could it ever sound so nice?
Commas hiding, giggles swell,
Each pause begins a secret spell.

With whispers floating, joined in play,
A riddle forms the words to say.
In silence, laughter sprouts and twirls,
Creating joy that wiggles, whirls.

Roots of Resilience

In the garden where gnomes play,
The weeds rise up, shouting hooray!
They dance in the breeze, quite a sight,
As long as the sunlight is just right.

The carrots are laughing, their tops in a twirl,
While cabbages gossip, oh what a whirl!
Each root finds a way to delight,
Creating a party from morning till night.

The daisies recount tales of their bloom,
While spuds sip on tea from a plastic cup room.
The soil's a disco, quite wild on the floor,
With ladybugs rolling, "Hey, give me some more!"

Oh, the laughter that sprouts from below,
As the broccoli teases the thyme, 'You're slow!'
With a wink, they unite in a friendly charade,
The garden of giggles—what a grand parade!

Hush of the Hollow

In the woods where the owls act quirky,
The silence tickles, feeling all jerky.
A squirrel drops acorns like a bad juggler,
While crickets hold concerts—mine's got a smuggler!

There's a brook chuckling, babbling away,
Mocking the missteps of frogs on display.
Each tree is a witness, arms crossed in cheer,
To the blunders of nature, oh, how sincere!

The shadows are giggling, a soft little tease,
As twilight creeps in, they dance in the breeze.
With whispers of mischief, they echo and sway,
In this hush, the boisterous creatures play!

Beneath the moon's light, all things seem bright,
As the laughter of night fills the heart with delight.
In this hollow of fun, no trouble betides,
Just nature's wild antics where laughter abides.

Serenity's Embrace

In a meadow where daisies pose so sweet,
The butterflies flounce about on tiny feet.
A bee whispers jokes to a sleepy old snail,
While the sun coaxes smiles, lifting the veil.

The breeze plays a tune on a flute made of grass,
Tickling the clouds that float high and pass.
With each gentle giggle, the flowers all sway,
Planting some humor to brighten the day.

The shadows are lazy, stretched out on the ground,
While a cricket's sweet serenade bounces around.
Even the stones, they chuckle in tune,
Caught up in the joy provided by June.

In the arms of this calm, fun sneaks right in,
With echoes of laughter like a mischievous grin.
Resting in peace, while the world spins its wheels,
This quiet's a riot, or so it reveals!

Subtle Movements

In the mist, where light tiptoes and plays,
The shadows are plotting their playful ways.
Kaleidoscope laughter jumps on the leaves,
As squirrels wear shades, swinging from eaves.

The mushrooms are winking, blushing with cheer,
While a hedgehog rolls by—'What's happening here?'
The ferns wave a flag in a soft little dance,
Encouraging critters to join in the prance.

Each ripple of water, a giggly retreat,
With fish flashing smiles in their underwater fleet.
Even the rocks feel a tickle beneath,
As nature decides to create quite the feast!

In these subtle movements, whimsy ignites,
With every small shuffle, the world's full of bites.
So come join this circus of soft, silly fun,
Where laughter's the language that shows we are one!

Serenity's Embrace

In the garden, a squirrel prances,
Chasing leaves with wild glances.
While daisies giggle, quite absurd,
Bumblebees hum a sweet, soft word.

A cactus wears a floppy hat,
As a timid snail does a slow chat.
They swap tales of the sun's warm tease,
While the pond just smiles, at ease.

The breeze is a jester, quite a clown,
Tickling the flowers, making them frown.
A butterfly flutters, quite loud and proud,
While the shadows check if it's allowed.

So laughter blooms where calm does stay,
Nature's quirks come out to play.
In every corner, joy takes flight,
In quiet corners, what a sight!

Bound by Nature's Silence

A frog in a pond wears a tiny crown,
While crickets compose a nighttime gown.
The moon peeks in, a curious guest,
To find the trees having a jest.

Old roots gossip in their ancient ways,
Trading secrets of long-lost days.
With mushrooms laughing in perfect glee,
While owls hoot, 'What's next for me?'

The wind rolls in, a ticklish tease,
Shaking leaves down from lofty trees.
Even the stones have a tale to tell,
As they chuckle, 'This stillness is swell!'

In nature's hush, silliness thrives,
Amongst the peaceful, the wiggly vibes.
A symphony played in the quiet of night,
Where chuckles bloom under starlit light.

In the Heart of a Still Moment

Lazily, the sun begins to yawn,
As sleepy flowers greet the dawn.
A caterpillar winks at me,
Saying, 'Just wait, I'll fly carefree!'

Grasshoppers play hide and seek,
While sleepy turtles take a peek.
They wave their heads, in unison sway,
In silent silliness, they display.

Pebbles giggle under sleepy feet,
As ants do the cha-cha, oh-so-sweet.
Nature's pause, a joyful spree,
Where stillness dances, endlessly.

So here we linger, no rush in sight,
As laughter stirs in the golden light.
In every quiet nook, we find,
The playful heart of nature, kind.

The Dance of Unbending Tranquility

In a park where the squirrels shuffle,
Chasing their tails with a great big chuckle.
The flowers wave in a comical line,
As bees do a jig, feeling quite fine.

A leaf whispered secrets to a stone,
While nearby, a dog sneezed, and a gnome groaned.
The frogs serenade, with a croaky song,
In harmony, the stillness, oh so strong.

A ladybug dons a polka-dot suit,
As the sun blinks in, a cute little brute.
The grass sways gently, with a chuckle so sly,
In this peaceful dance, even time passes by.

Sipping on calm like a warm cup of tea,
Nature giggles, 'Just let it be!'
With every moment, laughter springs,
In the cozy cradle that stillness brings.

Still Patches in a Chaotic World

In the midst of honks and shouts,
A cat naps on a windowsill,
Dreaming of mice, without a doubt,
While I try to pay my bill.

Socks that are missing, lost at sea,
Wandering far, who knows where?
Their journey's a mystery to me,
Perhaps they've gone to find fresh air.

The coffee pot gurgles a tune,
As I dance around my sleepy day,
But it keeps spilling way too soon,
Guess I'll be awake, come what may!

In chaos, we find a quiet laugh,
As the neighbor's dog brings back a shoe,
Each silly moment is the best half,
In a world that's wildly askew.

The Pause Before Dawn

Before the sun fills up the sky,
I trip on my own two feet,
Whispers of night begin to sigh,
As I search for something to eat.

The kettle whistles like a bird,
My toast jumps up like a clown,
In the calm, madness can be stirred,
As I spill jam all over my gown!

Cats stretch and yawn, in the dim light,
Planning their day of purring and play,
While I stumble into the bright,
Wondering what's for breakfast today.

The world gets quirky at this hour,
As I sip on coffee that burns my tongue,
Those gentle moments hold great power,
Even when morning's not yet sprung.

Silence Cradles the Night

In the hush of the evening tide,
Snoring dogs fill up the space,
While shadows of cats sway and glide,
Dreaming of chasing a mouse in a race.

Crickets play their nightly song,
Reminding me of dance class missed,
While the moonbeam finds where I belong,
In a cozy corner, lost in bliss.

Blankets are wrapped like a burrito,
While I search for the TV remote,
As quietness sparkles like a veto,
To the chaos of the day I wrote.

Laughter echoes in the night air,
With each bump of the old wooden floor,
In this space with no need to fare,
Serenity bursts through every door.

A Quiet Symphony of Solitude

With one shoe on and one shoe off,
I dance like no one's watching me,
In solitude, I might just scoff,
At how silly life can truly be.

The spoon slips from my hands with grace,
Landing right in the soup pot's dream,
A quiet symphony in this place,
As the cat decides to loudly scream!

Whispers of moments softly found,
Guide me to giggles and soft sighs,
In laughter's embrace, I'm unwound,
Life is a jest in disguise!

Each twist of fate brings a cheer,
As I trip on thoughts in my mind,
In solitude, the world feels near,
Happiness tangled, all defined.

Dewdrops of Silence

In a field where daisies dance,
A snail wears a hat, it's quite a chance.
It stops to ponder, in slow delight,
While a butterfly winks, mischief in sight.

The grass tickles toes, just like a tease,
As ants throw a party, with crumbs and cheese.
They pass the time, without a care,
While a ladybug spins, in the cool air.

A breeze whispers jokes, trees chuckle low,
While clouds share secrets we'll never know.
The shadows play tag, oh what a sight,
Nature's a comedian, day turns to night.

Murmurs from the Quiet Woods

In the woods where whispers roam,
A squirrel performs, stealing the show.
With acorns as props, it leaps with flair,
Leaves get the giggles; it's quite a scare!

The owls exchange puns, all in good fun,
While rabbits tell tales 'til the day is done.
A frog joins in with a ribbit so grand,
Leading the choral, they form a band.

The shadows sway under a giggly moon,
While crickets tap dance to a soft tune.
Even the rocks chuckle at all that they hear,
As nature's humor brings everyone cheer.

Tranquil Interstices

In the shades of calm, where giggles hide,
A beetle takes selfies, feeling quite spried.
"You've got a great angle!" the grass whispered low,
While the flowers all watch with a colorful glow.

The brook does a shuffle, splashes all around,
Tickling the toes of the ants on the ground.
They march in a line, with swagger and sway,
While a shy little fern watches them play.

The sun plays peek-a-boo, with clouds in the sky,
Tickling the leaves as it dances by.
The whole leafy ensemble, a whimsical scene,
As laughter erupts from the tiniest bean.

Illuminated Pauses

Under beams of light, where shadows conspire,
A cat naps away, dreaming of fire.
While lizards discuss the best sunning spots,
And chipmunks debate on whether to trot.

A playful breeze teases the branches about,
"Who's the queen of stillness?" it shouts with a pout.
The flowers all giggle, petals in bloom,
While the whispers of grasses begin to consume.

Tiny critters gather, in circles they spin,
Oh, the sage old turtle has no need for kin.
It watches with glee, a sage of the lot,
In a world full of laughter, it cares quite a lot.

The Calm Between Beats

In the silence, I hear a sneeze,
What was that? A ghost with allergies?
My goldfish swims in deep thought,
Wondering why it's never caught.

A cat naps on my empty chair,
Dreaming of mice without a care.
The clock ticks slow, it seems to grin,
Like it's laughing at my din.

I tried to dance without a sound,
But bumped my toe, fell to the ground.
The fridge hums a cheeky tune,
Even laughter takes its noon.

So here I sit without a frown,
In stillness, my chaos goes down.
Life's quirks are a song, quite neat,
Who knew quiet could be so sweet?

Veils of Tranquility

Beneath a blanket of soft, cool air,
A rubber duck takes a moment to stare.
The toaster belches crumbs like confetti,
As if the kitchen is a party, all ready.

A turtle slowly makes its stroll,
In a race against time—oh, what a goal!
The tea kettle whistles a quirky sound,
Is it celebrating or just feeling round?

The cat's plotting schemes quite sly,
With each paw step, it's a stealthy spy.
Meanwhile, I sip my cup so small,
In this serene chaos, I'm having a ball.

With laughter ringing like chimes on air,
I find solace in silly, without a care.
Moments pause, twist, and then release,
In tranquility's funny masterpiece.

Blossoms in Reflection

In the mirror, my hair does a dance,
Oh look, it's taken quite the chance!
A biscuit crumbles on my shirt,
Fashion statement: snack expert alert.

The plants gossip as they sway,
"Did you hear what the wind had to say?"
Sunlight filters through a leaf,
Bringing mischief, joy, and relief.

A squirrel rides by on a bike,
I swear it did a little hike.
Birds chirp gossip, from trees they call,
Each branch holds secrets, I love them all.

As I reflect on antics here,
With chuckles and giggles that I hold dear.
In breezy whispers, they softly flow,
Creating laughter in nature's show.

Shadows of the Unseen

In the corner, a shadow strikes a pose,
An umbrella taking a nap, who knows?
My slippers spring a dance routine,
While dust bunnies cheer from their unseen scene.

A noodle whispers from the pot,
"Hey, watch me twist—I'm quite the hotshot!"
The spoon winks at a mug with glee,
Together they conspire to brew some tea.

A couch potato's dream takes flight,
With popcorn clouds, oh what a sight!
It dreams of a world outside its box,
Where even the fridge dances in socks.

So let's raise a toast to the unseen,
In a world where silliness reigns supreme.
For in the shadows, joy may hide,
Just look around—let laughter be your guide!

Dreams Resting in Stillness

In corners where the dust bunnies play,
The dreams lie under a couch, tucked away.
Whispers of laughter from deep in the night,
Socks tell tales of their epic flight.

A cat naps hard, with dreams of great fish,
While mice in a corner plot for their wish.
Together they weave stories of glee,
In this realm where all simply must be.

In such quiet moments we find our great fate,
A toothbrush that sang, a half-eaten plate.
As time creeps by, we chuckle to see,
Life's little quirks are so silly and free.

So let the night linger, with its sneaky tune,
And dreamers will dance with the light of the moon.
When morning arrives with a push of a shoe,
We stand up, do a jig, and bid dreams adieu.

Nature's Silent Symphony

Amidst the trees, a squirrel plays jazz,
With acorns as drums, it's quite the pizzazz.
The breeze hums a tune that's oddly off-key,
As flowers tap dance, quite sprightly and free.

An owl nearby, in spectacles old,
Gathers the wisdom that nature has told.
While ants in a line march in perfect refrain,
Bickering softly about sunshine and rain.

The pond is a stage where frogs croak in style,
Each jump like a leap that brings laughter and guile.
The willows sway gently, adding their part,
To this quirky concert that tickles the heart.

In silence we chuckle, in stillness we cheer,
For nature's grand opera is perfectly clear.
So grab your popcorn and take a front row,
To this brilliant show where oddities glow.

Unraveled Threads

Once a sock was lost in the shuffle of clothes,
Seeking its duo, wherever it goes.
Threads of confusion, sewn neat and tight,
Now make up a tale that's awfully light.

A sweater with holes, quite tired of wear,
Wonders aloud, is this life really fair?
While buttons debate if it's time to retire,
Amid frayed edges, they gather their fire.

A scarf winds about with dramatic flair,
Telling the other threads, "Do you even care?"
Yet tangled up tight, they all laugh with glee,
At the shenanigans of fabricistry.

So in this great chaos of needle and thread,
They weave bits of laughter, each riddle unsaid.
For when the stitching is done and the humor had,
Fashion's just threads that make good dance mad.

The Solace of Seclusion

In a hammock's embrace, with the sun shining bright,
I ponder the mysteries of a squirrel's delight.
Does it plan its escape, or just wing it all?
While ants form a march, then stumble and fall.

A sunbeam finds pockets of warmth in the shade,
Where the grass grows tall, and the sunflowers fade.
They gossip in whispers, about bugs that parade,
While clouds overhead do a light-hearted charade.

As nature unfolds its absurd little charms,
A bee buzzing wildly, with no sense of qualms.
What joy it must be to flit here and there,
Yet dodge all the chores; do I dare to compare?

So in quiet repose, I sitcom my days,
With marveling chuckles in whimsical ways.
For seclusion's a stage, and laughter's the play,
In the theater of life, where humor holds sway.

Nature's Quiet Canvas

In shadows where daisies weave,
A butterfly sneezed, can you believe?
Amidst the calm, a squirrel slips,
While ants throw parties, doing backflips.

The rocks hold secrets, or so they say,
Birds exchange jokes in their own way.
Grasses giggle, tickled by breeze,
As worms check maps for hidden cheese.

Even the trees wear funny hats,
In the sun's glow, they all have chats.
A turtle debates speed, oh what a jest,
While crickets serenade, feeling blessed.

So let's embrace this tranquil show,
Where nature's chuckles help us grow.
In serene corners, laughter abounds,
Life's oddities echo in whispers and sounds.

The Poetry of Inactivity

Sitting still on a grassy mound,
The best ideas are nowhere found.
A snail writes poems with a tiny pen,
While a sloth ponders when to begin again.

Clouds float by in a lazy dream,
A bee stops to join a poet's theme.
Nature's lullaby, not a rush in sight,
As shadows dance in the soft moonlight.

Rocks read books under sunlit rays,
While all the flowers debate their days.
A grasshopper hums a tune so sweet,
On this couch of green, we take a seat.

So chuckle at time, let hours unfold,
As laughter lingers in stories retold.
In the art of doing nothing, we find,
Humor blossoms in the quiet grind.

Gentle Caress of Hours

Time crawls like a snail on a quest,
With no agenda, it knows no rest.
A clock hangs out, but its hands don't race,
As moments tiptoe in easy grace.

Lazily, the sun drapes itself bright,
While the cat naps, dreaming of flight.
A squirrel wearing glasses reads a book,
As daisies gather to share the look.

The brook chuckles with a soft gurgle,
While leaves play peekaboo in a swirl.
A frog tries its best to breakdance,
Whilst nature chuckles at every chance.

So let's toast to time's gentle embrace,
With a wink and a smile, it sets the pace.
In the quiet of hours, laughter ignites,
As stillness teems with delightful sights.

In the Wake of Stillness

In the wake of calm, a tale takes flight,
A worm recites jokes in the dim moonlight.
A toad croaks wisdom from the pond's edge,
While stars list their plans on a friendly pledge.

The grass sways softly, in rhythm they dance,
Each blade a partner in a silly chance.
A moth writes letters to a distant star,
Saying, 'Life's a hoot, let's raise the bar!'

The trees nod knowingly, secrets they share,
As twigs fall down without a care.
Even the drifts of snow crack a smile,
In laughter's embrace, we linger a while.

So here's to the charming stillness we bask,
In naps and giggles, no questions to ask.
For in gentle moments, we find delight,
As nature chuckles beneath the moonlight.

Still Waters Run Deep

In a pond where ducks just lounge,
A rubber duck makes quite a frown.
It dreams of waves and ocean bliss,
Yet sways in place, can't move, oh this!

Beneath the surface, fish do plot,
To leap and twist, or not, oh not!
They roll their eyes at the old log,
As it transforms into a frog.

The lily pads are quite the scene,
They gossip 'bout the frog's routine.
'He hops around like he's a star,
But doesn't know just where we are!'

A wise old turtle sighs and grins,
'Life's slow lane has its silly spins.
We linger here, the laugh is grand,
While time slips softly through our hands.

Petals on a Gentle Breeze

A petal danced upon the air,
It twirled and dipped without a care.
'Look at me, I'm such a float!'
It laughed, 'I'm free as any boat!'

But just behind, a bee did hum,
And said, 'Dear petal, you're so dumb!
You're caught in my dandelion glue,
Now you can't breeze, it's sad but true!'

The petal huffed, 'I'll simply fly!'
But the bee buzzed, 'Oh, try, oh try!'
'You aim for freedom but aren't so bright,
You're just a snack in my bold flight!'

Yet still it tugged, and still it played,
Chasing the breeze, unafraid.
'This sticky mess will make me wise,
At least my dance will win the prize!'

Moments in Between

In the middle of a light rain,
A squirrel slipped and took the stain.
It shook its tail, then took a dive,
A splashy leap, like it's alive!

A puddle formed, called 'Jump right in!'
But the reindeer laughed, 'Where's the win?
You're just a fluff in muddy woes,
With soggy socks and water woes!'

The ants stood in a silly line,
They scuttled quick, their dance divine.
'Between the drops, we form a chain,
Come join the fun, stop all the pain!'

So squirrel leaped, in silly glee,
And danced with ants, a jubilee.
While raindrops played a light encore,
In joyous moments, they explored!

The Art of Pausing

A cat sits still on a sunny ledge,
With one paw up, it makes a pledge.
'I'll sit right here and take my time,
To nap and dream, it's simply prime!'

A dog trots by, with wagging tail,
'Why don't you move? You're turning pale!'
The cat just yawns, a stretch so slow,
'I'm perfecting the art of 'no go'!'

With every meow, the clock tilts tight,
As birds fly in, 'What a sight!'
'You snooze away, while we take flight,
But pause this, cat, you're out of sight!'

Yet, in that sunbeam, dreams do bloom,
As shadows dance across the room.
In stillness, laughter finds its grace,
For moments pause, we take our place.

Stillness in a Swaying World

In a world that twirls and spins,
Even the daisies wear silly grins.
They sway to the beat of a breezy tune,
With dance moves that make the sun laugh at noon.

The grass does the wobble, the trees do the twist,
In the chaos of motion, they can't resist.
A squirrel with a hat keeps stealing the show,
While the flowers just giggle, 'Oh, look at him go!'

The pond joins the party, its ripples do leap,
With ducks performing dives, oh so deep.
Fish wear tiny shoes, and frogs jump in line,
Holding a disco of laughter divine.

So when life gets hectic and throws you a spin,
Remember the daisies, where silliness begins.
In this swirling world, find joy in the light,
And join the sweet dance, let your worries take flight.

Silent Tendrils

In corners where shadows play peek-a-boo,
Whiskers of tendrils grow out of the blue.
They reach for the cookies, they stretch for some cake,
Silently plotting their sugary break.

With whispers of giggles, they tickle the air,
As they dance on the counter without any care.
The spoons hold a meeting, the cups roll their eyes,
'Look at those sneaky vines!' they whisper in surprise.

A grape vine in purple wears glasses so thick,
Claiming that recipes come from the stick.
"Come join the fun!" they call to a squash,
Just don't bring your friends, or it'll be a squash squash!

So if you hear rustling from kitchen to hall,
Just watch for those tendrils, and answer their call.
In silent adventures where mischief is done,
You'll find laughter sprouting – it's all just for fun!

Whispers in the Wind

The leaves tell secrets in breezy delight,
Like gossiping friends on a warm summer night.
"Did you see that spider? He spun quite the show!
His web's a grand ballroom for a bug ballet pro!"

The winds carry chuckles from tree to tree,
As dandelions drift, wild and carefree.
The clouds eavesdrop closely, their shapes start to tease,
"Oh look, it's a bunny! No, wait, it's a breeze!"

While daisies wave wildly, they giggle and share,
"Did you hear the grasshopper bragging out there?
He thinks he's a singer – on pitch and on key,
But we all know he's just chirping with glee!"

So listen closely when the winds start to play,
For tales of the forest are swirling away.
In the whispers of nature, humor's a vibe,
Join in the laughter, let your spirit imbibe!

Echoes of Quietude

In a creek where the pebbles like to have fun,
They echo each splash, like laughter begun.
The stones hold a party, their rounds never end,
As frogs chant in chorus, "Come join us, my friend!"

With ripples of chuckles that dance in the light,
Every moment a giggle, a joyous bite.
The turtles are judging, but in good buzzing cheer,
Watching the shenanigans, nibbling on their geese gear.

The owls hoot with laughter at folly so grand,
As shadows perform in a carefree band.
"Who needs to be serious?" the branches decide,
"Let's roll with the giggles, let's shake off our pride!"

So wander the echoes where laughter takes place,
In the calm of the forest, there's humor to chase.
With each little ripple, with each gentle sound,
You'll find that the quiet has joy all around.

The Harmony of Motionless Dreams

In the land where stillness wins,
A squirrel debates its morning spins.
The grass whispers, 'Quiet! It's time!'
While daisies giggle in perfect rhyme.

A snail dreams of sprinting there,
As ladybugs twirl without a care.
The clouds above snore, soft and round,
In this sleepy town, no pace is found.

Hiccups of laughter bounce in air,
A turtle raises a lazy dare.
With every blink, a game of hide,
In dreams where motion cannot bide.

Oh, the fun in this frozen place,
Where time forgets its bustling race.
A pogo stick rests, not even one jump,
In harmony, they all just slump.

Roots of Reflection in Silent Soil

Beneath the ground, a joke takes root,
Earthworms chuckle in their mud suit.
Rocks lay still, but they're not shy,
Cracking puns as the breezes sigh.

The potatoes plot their grand parade,
While radishes muse on the jokes they've made.
Roots in a tangle, they silently shout,
'We may be stuck, but we'll never pout!'

A carrot dreams of dance and sway,
But moves like it's on a holiday.
They giggle in dirt with joy so sweet,
In the silence, their laughter's neat.

Underneath, where the soil is deep,
The laughter of roots finds joy to keep.
Nature's whispers, a troublesome crew,
With silent giggles shared by few.

Undisturbed Horizons of Thought

Thought balloons float in the calm blue,
Each one a funny idea or two.
A thought to share, but silence reigns,
As they quip and giggle, tied with chains.

The peaks of pride sit quiet and high,
While clouds below settle with a sigh.
A pebble jokes of a leap it won't,
'Why jump when stillness is the front?'

As winds carry whispers that tickle ears,
Laughter peeks through the drapes of fears.
The sun snickers down on the ocean's crest,
In stillness, thoughts wear their Sunday best.

In a world where hustle holds no sway,
Mirth lingers in the sun's soft ray.
Each horizon quietly winks at night,
In the still drone of a soft moonlight.

The Essence of Paused Time

Time sits back with a cozy drink,
Playing chess with shadows, not a blink.
The clock's hands halt for a lazy chat,
As the seconds giggle, 'What's up with that?'

An hourglass checks its sandy flow,
'Have you seen my grains? They're too slow!'
In every tick is a silly play,
Where moments stretch like they're on holiday.

Laughter echoes in the quiet dome,
A pause that feels like a warm home.
Backwards and forwards, time does the twist,
In this stillness, it's hard to resist.

Oh, the rhythm of this gentle trap,
Where life is a great, unhurried nap.
Wrapped in a blanket of carefree rhyme,
Here, even clocks lose track of time.

Gossamer Threads of Peace

In a world where cats conspire,
To nap atop the warmest chair,
They dream of fish and mice on fire,
While we just wonder how they dare.

Suspended in a fuzzy haze,
The toast, it pops and sings aloud,
We laugh at life's bizarre displays,
As crumbs collect beneath the cloud.

Lemonade spills from too much zest,
A bee now dances with a hat,
We're all just trying to feel blessed,
Yet somehow get wrapped up in chat.

So here we float on puffy chairs,
Beneath the sun's eternal rays,
In laughter, life just brings us snares,
But oh, the joy in silly ways!

A Breath Between Heartbeats

In one brief moment we all freeze,
Waiting for the pizza guy,
The clock ticks on with playful tease,
While we debate if we should cry.

Socks that don't match start a trend,
And noodles dance like they're on show,
Friends argue which ones are the best,
While silence grows, as tempers flow.

We pause to savor every bite,
As laughter bubbles in the air,
Each meal becomes a comical sight,
With sauce that splatters everywhere.

So take a breath, and laugh out loud,
In every moment, joy is found,
Chasing the silliness around,
For life's a stage with a big crowd!

The Art of Waiting Softly

A line for coffee stretches long,
The barista hums a catchy tune,
As customers swap tales of wrong,
And giggles brighten morning gloom.

We count the quirky cups around,
With faces drawn in whipped-up cream,
Each sip a newfound joy unbound,
As friendships blossom, dream by dream.

Patience becomes a playful game,
As donuts cause a joyful sprawl,
With sprinkles dancing just the same,
We laugh until we start to fall.

So here we wait in gentle bliss,
With frothy drinks and tales to weave,
In every pause, a little kiss,
Of humor, joy, and tricks up sleeve!

Hidden Currents of Rest

A quiet park with ducks in line,
Each waddling tale a comic show,
As passersby sip on sweet wine,
While squirrels plot a nutty throw.

The wind whispers jokes to the trees,
As shadows dance upon the ground,
While our thoughts drift like autumn leaves,
With laughter echoing all around.

And every bench becomes a stage,
As friends recount their wildest dreams,
Turning boredom into a page,
With stories bursting at the seams.

So in this calm, let spirits rise,
For humor lives where stillness lies,
Where every sigh becomes a cheer,
And joy brings laughter year to year!

Threads of Quietude

In gardens where the gnomes all grin,
A snail's race begins, let the fun begin!
The daisies gossip, petals spread wide,
While dandelions dance with a fluffy stride.

A ladybug dons her polka dot best,
In the world of bugs, she's better than the rest!
With ants on a mission, determined and spry,
They hold a parade, oh my, oh my!

Swells of Contemplation

The cat on the windowsill ponders a leep,
For why chase the mouse when you could just sleep?
A goldfish's bubble is bursting with thought,
Why swim in circles when trouble's not sought?

A squirrel does yoga, as nimble as can be,
With poses so silly, he starts to feel free.
While shadows of clouds play tag in the sky,
Who knew quiet moments could shatter and fly?

Echoes Among the Pines

The trees gossip softly beneath the bright sun,
While squirrels debate which acorn is fun.
The rustling leaves share a quirky old tale,
Of a hedgehog's journey on a fateful snail trail.

A bird chirps a tune with a comical flair,
As pinecones tumble down, do they have hearts, beware!
Nature's own choir, each note a delight,
Where laughter and echoes take flight in the night.

Quietude's Embrace

A duck wears a crown, with elegance grand,
Paddling around as if it's all planned.
The frogs keep the beat, with plops in the pond,
Creating rhythms that stretch far and beyond.

The moon tries to wink, yet he's caught in the haze,
While crickets compose their nocturnal praise.
In the heart of the calm, where chuckles arise,
Life's whimsical moments dance under the skies.

Echoing Through the Trees

In the woods where whispers play,
A squirrel talks to leaves each day.
The breeze chuckles in delight,
As branches dance, a funny sight.

A rabbit giggles, hops with glee,
While birds chirp jokes from their tree.
The shadows wink and roll around,
Nature's laughter is profound.

A cheeky fox with playful prance,
Invites the deer to join the dance.
The acorns drop like chuckled cheers,
Echoing softly through the years.

In this calm, a party brews,
With nature sharing all its views.
So grab a leaf, join in the fun,
Together we'll laugh 'til day is done.

Stillness Takes Root

Beneath the quiet, roots will chat,
With quirky jokes, they chatter scat.
A worm pipes in with silly tales,
While slugs laugh softly, leaving trails.

The flowers nod with rosy cheer,
As daisies tease the busy deer.
In stillness where the chuckles bloom,
Whispers dance and dispel the gloom.

A pine tree sways with secret glee,
Tickling the breeze, a comedy.
While dandelions prank the wind,
In this calm space, laughter's pinned.

So here we sit, roots intertwine,
With nature's humor, so divine.
In every stillness, fun can grow,
A secret world we all can know.

Harmonies of the Heart

In a meadow, tunes abound,
With bees who hum a funny sound.
A butterfly plays hide and seek,
While laughing flowers wax unique.

The grass joins in, a vibrant choir,
Tickles the earth with flares of fire.
Each laugh a note upon the breeze,
A melody made, with perfect ease.

The trees clap hands with leafy grace,
While shadows dance in playful chase.
A giggling brook sings with delight,
Under the stars, twinkling bright.

In this concert, joy takes flight,
Where nature's laughter feels just right.
So let your heart join in the song,
In the funny moments, we belong.

Fleeting Flickers of Peace

A candle flickers, shadows clap,
With each small glow, the gnomes zap.
A wink from light, a playful tease,
As whispers float upon the breeze.

The night takes hold, and stars peek in,
While crickets laugh, they slowly spin.
A firefly winks, it wobbles past,
A tiny glow, yet shines so fast.

In fleeting moments, peace does bloom,
With silly grins that chase the gloom.
The nightingale sings out a jest,
In quiet chaos, we find rest.

So let us bask in peace so fleet,
With laughter at our silly feet.
In the calm, we'll dance, we'll play,
Finding fun in night and day.

Lullabies of the Liminal

In the space between snacks and dreams,
Mice hold concerts with tiny screams.
Tea cups dance on window sills,
While the kettle's off on frolicking thrills.

Socks hang out, their colors a mess,
On the line of glee, they claim they're the best.
Pillows giggle at secrets they hear,
Whispering jokes that only they cheer.

The clock ticks sideways in a polka dot suit,
Counting the moments with a wobbly boot.
Curtains flutter like they've lost a bet,
In the lounge of laughter, no need to fret.

Here in this middle, where silliness reigns,
Even the cat is breaking chains.
With cartwheels of joy, they prance around,
In the lullaby of lost and found.

Quiet Gardens

In the garden where gnomes wear shades,
Moles plot schemes as the sun slowly fades.
A bee plays hide and seek by the rose,
While the daisies giggle at their garden woes.

Squirrels mix nuts with a dash of cheese,
Beneath the old oak, they toss in the breeze.
Flowers whisper tales of the worms below,
Making friends with beetles—quite the show!

A breeze carries laughter and sweet perfume,
While shadows do cha-cha in full bloom.
Even the thorns wear a cheeky grin,
As they craft their pricks with a bow and a spin.

Oh, the quiet tales this place can tell,
Of playful antics where all creatures dwell.
Where blossoms blink twice just for fun,
And calmness dances, a joke just begun.

Ephemeral Whispers

Ears bend low to secrets unheard,
As ants compose an absurd little word.
Butterflies barter their jokes in the air,
Trading giggles with a dash of flair.

Pebbles bounce gently from step to step,
In a game of checkers where mushrooms prep.
The sky spills giggles like confetti on grass,
While clouds trade winks as the moments pass.

Every whisper twirls in a playful jig,
As the moon dons sneakers and does a big gig.
Even the stars twinkle with glee,
Spreading laughter through spaces so free.

Oh, ephemeral tales drift on the breeze,
With every tickle, laughter finds ease.
Sharing sweet nothings, they slyly concur,
In the soft spoken language of laughter's motor purr.

The Softness of Solitude

In gentle corners, where shadows recline,
Llamas in pajamas share bottled sunshine.
Tea leaves gossip with a flick of flair,
In the softness of quiet—what a rare affair!

A lone cat dons a detective hat,
Searching for secrets in a cozy spat.
Whiskers twitch as the clock starts to yawn,
While the soup pot hums an old country song.

The blanket folds in a snug little heap,
While spoons settle down for a very good sleep.
Even the dust motes begin to dance,
In the tranquil embrace of this blissful chance.

Oh, the delightful mischief in being alone,
As the world whispers softly, a gentle tone.
With laughter in silence, and joy in the air,
In this quilt of solitude, all hearts can share.

Pondering by the Still Waters

A frog thinks deep by the pond's side,
It ponders life, and chooses to hide.
With ripples forming, a fish swims through,
"Is that my lunch?" it wonders too.

The lilies laugh, they swish and sway,
"Who knew reflection would make us play?"
Butterflies giggle in the warm sun,
And whisper tales of their day of fun.

The breeze plays tag with the reeds so high,
Each wave a laugh, a playful sigh.
Two ducks quack jokes while they float by,
As if the water holds secrets nigh.

Yet here I sit, just passing the time,
Observing nature, all in mime.
As life unfolds its quirky plot,
I chuckle softly, forgetting the thought.

Veils of Time in Hushed Corners

In shadows where the whispers thrive,
Time tiptoes in, so sly and jive.
A clock that's late, it strikes with glee,
"Who needs to hurry? Just drink some tea!"

Dust bunnies dance like it's a ball,
With fluffy gowns, they laugh and call.
"Why rush outside when we can twirl,
In this cozy corner, let's give it a whirl?"

Old photos peek from their picture frames,
Muttering secrets and forgotten games.
"Remember when?" they slyly grin,
As time giggles softly, wearing a spin.

So let the world spin fast and wide,
I'll stay here with the giggles inside.
In corners hushed, where silence plays,
I'm loving these sweet, timeless days.

Where Silence Blooms

In gardens where the quiet grows,
A daisy whispers, "Shhh, it knows!"
Bees droning softly, stammer and stall,
"Is this pollen or just a ball?"

The trees wear silence like a cloak,
While squirrels plot over acorns, bespoke.
"Could we play hide and seek with the sun?
Who knew that stillness could be such fun?"

Roses blush from the gentle hush,
No need for daisies to rush, rush, rush.
Each petal giggles with silent glee,
"Just stopping to smell the calm's a key!"

So here's to blossoms that stand so still,
With laughter among them, a joyous thrill.
In the quiet spaces, life finds its way,
Where silence blooms, we dance and play.

The Stillness Beneath the Surface

A fish thinks deep beneath the wave,
Its silent world, quite the enclave.
"Is that a whale, or just my friend?
What a fishy tale, let's not pretend!"

Corals giggle in the great blue sea,
"A still life here, come have some tea!"
Sleepy turtles glide with a flair,
"Let's nap for ages, we haven't a care."

An octopus dances, arms in a twist,
"Who says I can't?" as he swirls and lists.
With colors flashing like a party's tag,
He laughs in bubbles—what a colorful brag!

The surface above may be swift and loud,
But underneath, life wears a shroud.
Where humor floats and stillness flies,
Life's wacky wonders hide in disguise.

A Dance in Silence

In a room full of chatter, like fish in a bowl,
A chair starts to jiggle, it's taking a stroll.
The cat joins the party, with grace and with flair,
But trips on a dustbin, flies high in the air.

The clock's quite amused, it ticks with a grin,
While the rug does a tango, it's twirling with sin.
Side tables are wobbling, unsure of their place,
As everyone laughs at this chaotic grace.

Calm Currents

The toaster's been silent, not a crumb in sight,
But it pops up a bagel, like it's ready to fight.
The fridge hums a tune, oh so cool and smooth,
While the coffee pot gurgles, it's found its groove.

The plants sway gently, they're grooving with ease,
While the dishwasher joins in, a symphonic tease.
And just when it's quiet, the blender goes wild,
Mixing chaos and laughter, like a mischievous child.

www.ingramcontent.com/pod-product-compliance
Lightning Source LLC
Chambersburg PA
CBHW051640160426
43209CB00004B/727